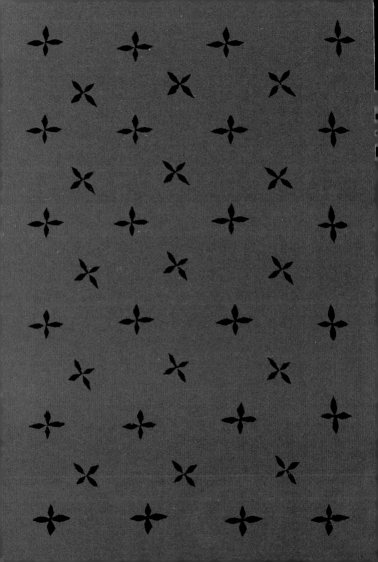

a little book of

Celtic Verse

Compiled by W A Ross

Illustrated by Angela McCormick

Appletree Press

First published by
The Appletree Press Ltd
19-21 Alfred Street
Belfast BT2 8DL

A catalogue record for this book is
available from the British Library

ISBN 0-86281-603-3

9 8 7 6 5 4 3 2 1

Introduction

The poems in this collection come from Gaelic (Scots and Irish), Welsh and Breton. Most of them have been translated into English more than once. The nineteenth century was the great era of tracking down Celtic verse and of translating it. We have used a number of nineteenth-century sources for this collection, but have occasionally adapted or modernised the translations.

We hope that this little collection will enable readers to appreciate the range of Celtic poetry, its topics, its many moods and modes. History can tell us the facts of a people, but their poetry goes a long way towards revealing their soul. The time-span is a great one, from the pre-Christian era to the eighteenth century, but the continuity of Celtic culture and the oral tradition give unity to the collection.

Deirdre's Farewell to Alba

Glen Etive! O, Glen Etive!
There I raised my earliest house;
Beautiful its woods on rising
Where the sun fell on Glen Etive.

Glen Orchy! O, Glen Orchy!
The straight glen of smooth ridges;
No man of the age was so joyful
As Naois in Glen Orchy.

Glenlaidhe! O, Glenlaidhe!
I used to sleep by its soothing murmurs;
Fish, and flesh of wild boar and badger
Was my repast in Glenlaidhe.

Glendaruadh! O, Glendaruadh!
I love each man of its inheritance;
Sweet the noise of the cuckoo on bending
    bow,
On the hill above Glendaruadh.

Glenmasan! O, Glenmasan!
High its herbs, fair its boughs;
Solitary was the place of our repose,
On grassy Invermasan.

Ossian's Lament

Long was last night in cold Elphin,
More long is tonight on its weary way.
Though yesterday seemed to me long and ill,
Yet longer still was this dreary day.

And long for me is each hour new-born,
Stricken, sad and smitten with grief
For the hunting lands and the Fenian bands,
And the long-haired, generous Fenian chief.

I hear no music, I find no feast,
I slay no beast from my prancing steed,
I bestow no gold, I am poor and old,
I am sick and cold, without wine or mead.

I court no more, and I hunt no more,
These were before my great delight.
I cannot slay, and I take no prey;
Weary the day and long the night.

No heroes come in battle array,
No game I play; there is nought to win.
I swim no stream with my men of might;
Long is the night in cold Elphin.

Ask, O Patrick, thy God of grace,
To tell me the place he will place me in,
And save my soul from the Ill One's might,
For long is tonight in cold Elphin.

St Columba on Iona

Delightful would it be to
   me
  From a rock pinnacle
  to trace
Continually
  The Ocean's face:
That I might watch the
   heaving waves
  Of noble force
To God the Father chant their staves
  Of the earth's course.
That I might mark its level strand,
  To me no lone distress,
That I might mark the sea-birds' wondrous
   band –
  Sweet source of happiness.
That I might hear the sounding billows thunder
  On the rough beach.
That by my holy church side I might ponder

Their mighty speech;
Or watch surf-skimming
    gulls the dark shoal
        follow
    With joyful scream,
Or giant ocean monsters
    spout and wallow,
    Wonder supreme!
That I might well observe
    of ebb and flood
    All cycles therein;
And that my mystic name might be for good
    But *Cul-ri Erin.**
That gazing toward her on my heart might fall
    A full contrition,
That I might then bewail my evils all,
    Though hard the admission;
That I might bless the Lord who all things
        orders
    For their great good.
The countless hierarchies through Heaven's

---

* Literally, "back turned to Ireland"

bright borders –
  Land, strand and flood.
That I might search all books and in their
    chart
  Find my soul's calm;
Now kneel before the Heaven of my heart,
  Now chant a psalm;
Now meditate upon the King of Heaven,
  Chief of the Holy Three;
Now ply my work by no compulsion driven,
  What greater joy could be?
Now picking dulse upon the rocky shore,
  Now fishing eager on,
Now furnishing food unto the starving poor
  In hermitage anon.
The guidance of the King of Kings
  Has been vouchsafed unto me;
If I keep watch beneath His wings
  No evil shall undo me.

The Scribe

For weariness my hand
   writes ill,
My small sharp quill
   runs rough and slow;
Its slender beak with
   failing craft
Gives forth its draught
   of dark-blue flow.

And yet God's blessed wisdom gleams
And streams beneath my fair brown palm,
As the quick jets of holly ink
The letters link of prayer or psalm.

So still my dripping pen I take
And make my mark on parchment white,
Unceasing, at some rich man's call,
Till wearied all am I tonight.

Crinog

(A Celtic monk's lament for his soul-sister)

Crinog of melodious song,
   No longer young, but bashful-eyed,
As when we roved Niall's northern land,
   Hand-in-hand or side by side.

Peerless maid, whose looks brimmed o'er
   With the lovely lore of Heaven,
By whom I slept in dreamless joy,
   A gentle boy of summers seven.

We dwelt in Banva's* broad domain,
   Without one stain of soul or sense;
While still mine eye flashed forth on thee
   Affection free of all offence.

*Ireland

To meet thy counsel quick and just,
  Our faithful trust responsive springs:
Better thy wisdom's searching force
  Than any smooth discourse with kings.

In sinless sisterhood with men,
  Four times, since then, thou hast been bound:
Yet not one rumour of ill-fame
  Against thy name has travelled round.

At last, their weary wanderings o'er,
  To me once more thy footsteps tend;
The gloom of age makes dark thy face,
  Thy life of grace draws near its end.

O faultless one, O very dear,
  Unstinted welcome here is thine.
Hell's haunting dread I ne'er shall feel,
  So thou art kneeling by my side.

Thy blessed fame shall ever bide,
  For far and wide thy feet have trod.
Could we their saintly track descry
  We yet should see the Living God.

You leave a pattern and bequest
  To all who rest upon the earth –
A life-long lesson to declare
  Of earnest prayer the precious worth.

God grant us peace and joyful love!
  And may the face of Heaven's King
Beam on us when we leave behind
  Our bodies blind and withering.

The Monk and his White Cat

Pangar, my white cat, and I
Silent ply our special crafts;
Hunting mice his one pursuit,
Mine to shoot keen spirit shafts.

For me no pleasure can exceed
Reading, absorbed in some rare book;
Yet white Pangar, at his play
Offers me no jealous look.

Thus together in one cell
Our time is spent – and far from dull;
Each one at his private task,
Finds that his life is rich and full.

See Pangar pounce upon his mouse,
With claws and jaws contrive the kill;
While I a meaning subtly framed
Hold in mind with studious thrill.

Now his green and lambent gaze
Surveys in hope the hollow wall;
My dimmer vision also seeks
To pierce the dark and see the whole.

Pangar springs with fearsome joy
To seize his prey in talons keen;
Problems difficult and dear
I stalk, and wisdom hope to glean.

Crossing not each other's will,
Diverse still, yet still allied,
Following each his own lone ends,
Constant friends we here abide.

Pangar, master of his art,
Plays his part in supple youth,
While I sedately strive to clear
Shadows from the light of Truth.

Hospitality

1
Whether my house is dark or bright,
I close it not on any wight,
Lest Thou, the King of Stars so great,
Should shut me out from Heaven's gate.

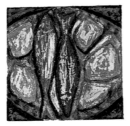

2
If from a guest who shares thy board,
Thy dearest dainty thou shalt hoard,
Not just thy guest, O never doubt it,
But Mary's Son shall go without it.

The Church Bell in the Night

Sweet little bell, sweet little bell,
Struck long and well upon the wind,
I'd rather tryst with thee tonight
Than any maiden light of mind.

Moling Sang This

When I with the old consort
Jest and sport they straight lay by;
When with frolic youth I'm flung,
Maddest of the young am I.

Advice to a Pilgrim

Unto Rome thou woulds't attain?
Great the toil is, small the gain,
If the King thou seek'st therein,
Travel not with thee from Erin.

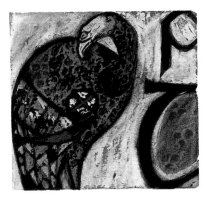

The Enchanted Valley

I will go where lilies blow
   And linger by the languid streams,
Within that vale where jewels glow;
    Where bright-winged dreams flit to and
      fro,
I long its magic peace to know.

Beware! Beware that vale so fair!
   A hollow phantom you will be –
Bereft alike of joy and care,
   You hunger for life's burden there
And ever cry, "Beware, beware!"

The Song of Fionn

May-day, delightful time. How beautiful the
   colour.
The blackbirds sing their full tune. Would that
   Laeg were here!
The cuckoos call in constant strains. How
   welcome is the noble
Brilliance of the changing season. On the margin
   of the branchy woods,
   The summer swallows skim the stream; swift
   horses seek the pool:
The heather spreads her long hair out; pale
   bog-myrtle thrives;
The sea is lulled to calm, flowers cover the
   earth.

The March of the Faerie Host

In well-planned battle array,
Ahead of their fair chieftain,
They march wielding blue spears,
White, curly-headed bands.

They scatter the armies of the foe,
They ravage every land,
Splendidly they march to battle
Impetuous, glamorous, avenging host!

No wonder that their strength be great:
Sons of kings and queens are one and all.
On all their heads are set
Beautiful manes of yellow-gold.

Their bodies comely, smooth,
Their eyes bright, blue-starred,
Pure crystal their teeth,
Thin their red lips:

Good they are at man-slaying.

The Outlaw's Song

"Who is that without
With voice like a sword,
That batters my bolted door?"

"I am Eamonn an Chnuic,
Cold, weary and wet
From long walking mountains and glens."

"O dear and bright love,
What would I do for you
But cover you with a skirt of my dress.
For shots full thick
Are raining on you,
And together we may be slaughtered!"

"Long am I out
Under snows, under frost,
Without comradeship with any,
My team unyoked,

My fallow unsown,
And they lost to me entirely;
Friend I have none
– I am heavy for that –
That would shelter me later or early,
And so I must go
East over the sea,
Since 'tis there I have no kindred."

The Sword Dance

Blood, wine and glee,
Sun, to you –
Blood, wine and glee!

Chorus
  Fire, fire, steel, O steel!
  Fire, fire! Steel and fire!
  Oak! Oak, earth and waves!
  Waves, oak, earth and oak!

Glee of dance and song,
And battle-throng –
Battle, dance and song!

Chorus

Let the sword-blades swing
In a ring –
Let the sword-blades swing!

Chorus

Song of the blue steel,
Death to feel –
Song of the blue steel!

Chorus

Fight, in which the sword
Is Lord –
Fight of the fell sword!

Chorus

Sword, you mighty king
Of battle's ring –
Sword, you mighty king!

Chorus

With the rainbow's light
Be you bright –
With the rainbow's light!

Fire, fire, steel, o steel!
Fire, fire! Steel and fire!
Oak! Oak, earth and waves!
Waves, oak, earth and oak!

I Am Watching my Young Calves Sucking

I am watching my young calves sucking:
Who are you that would put me out of of my
   luck?
Can I not be walking, can I not be walking,
Can I not be walking on my own farm-lands?

I will not for ever go back before you;
If I must needs be submissive to you, great is
   my grief;
If I cannot be walking, if I cannot be walking,
If I cannot be walking on my own farm-lands.

Little heed I pay, and 'tis little my desire,
Your fine blue cloak and your bright birds'
   plumes,
If I cannot be walking, if I cannot be walking,
If I cannot be walking on my own farm-lands!
There is a day coming, it is plain to my eyes,

When there will not be among us the mean
   likes of you;
But each will be walking, each will be
   walking,
Wherever he will, on his own farm-land.

The Yarrow

I will pluck the yarrow fair,
That kindlier shall be my face,
That more warm shall be my lips,
That more chaste shall be my speech,
Be my speech the beams of the sun,
Be my lips the sap of the strawberry.

May I be an isle in the sea,
May I be a hill on the shore,
May I be a star in the dark time,
May I be a staff to the weak:
Wound can I every man,
Wound can no man me.

What is Love?

A love much-enduring through a year is
   my love,
It is grief in the heart,
It is stretching of strength beyond its bounds,
It is the four quarters of the world,
It is the highest height of heaven,
It is breaking of the neck,
It is battle with a spectre,
It is drowning with water,
It is a race against heaven,
It is champion-deeds beneath the sea,
It is wooing the echo;
So is my love, and my passion,
And my devotion to her to whom I gave
   them.

Fairy Song

O little Morag
A-climbing bens,
Descending glens,
A-climbing bens,
O little Morag
A-climbing bens,
Tired you are
– And the calves lost.

Song of the River-Sprite Nigheag

I am washing the shrouds of the fair men
Who are going out but never shall come in;
The death-dirge of the ready-handed men
Who shall go out, seek peril and fall.

I am lustring the linen of the fair men
Who shall go out in the morning early,
Upon the well-shod grey steeds
And shall not return in season due.

from **A Song of Exile**

I sit on a knoll,
All sorrowful and sad,
And I look on the grey sea
In mistiness clad,
And I brood on strange chances
That drifted me here,
Where Scarba and Jura
And Islay lie near.

Where Scarba and Jura
And Islay are near;
Grand land of rough mountains,
I wish thee good cheer.
I wish young Sir Norman
On mainland and islands
To be named with proud honour
First chief in the Highlands!

To be praised with proud honour,
First chief in the Highlands,
For wisdom and valour
In far and in nigh lands;
For mettle and manhood,
There's none may compare,
With the handsome Macleod
Of the princeliest air.

And the blood in his veins
Proclaims him the heir
Of the kings of Lochlann;
It flows rich and rare.
Each proud earl in Alba
Is knit with his line,
And Erin shakes hands with him
Over the brine.

And Erin shakes hands with him
Over the brine;
Brave son of brave father,
The pride of his line.
In camp and in council
Whose virtue was seen,
Whose purse was as free
As his claymore was keen.

The Calends of Winter

The Calends of Winter are come; the grain
Grows hard; the dead leaf drops in
  the rain;
Though the stranger bid thee, turn
  not again.

The Calends of Winter: about the hearth
Draw the gossips close, as storm holds the
  earth;
Now many a secret spills in the mirth.

The Calends of Winter: forgot in the
  cold
The tale the Calends of Summer told –
What the cuckoo sang to the black
  bird bold.

The Calends of Winter: the night falls soon,
Black as the raven; the afternoon
Declines to evening without a tune.

The Calends of Winter are come. The heath
Is bare where it was burnt. The breath
Of the oxen smokes. The old await death.

The Fairy-king's Call

O Befind, wilt thou come with me
To the wondrous land of melody?
The crown of their head like the primrose
    fair,
Their bodies below as the colour of snow.

There in that land is no *mine* or *thine*;
White the teeth there, eyebrows black,
Brilliant the eyes – great is the host –
And each cheek the hue of the foxglove.

How heady so ever the ale of Inis Fàl,
More intoxicating the ale of the Great Land;
A marvel among lands, the land of which I
    speak;
No young man there enters upon old age.

Like the purple of the plain each neck,
Like the ousel's egg the colour of the eye;
Though fair to the sight are the plains of Fàl,
They are a desert to him who knows the
    Great Plains.

We behold every one on every side,
And none beholds us;
The gloom of Adam's sin it is
Conceals us from their reckoning.

O woman, if thou wilt come among my
strong people,
A golden crown shall grace thy head;
Fresh swine-flesh, new milk and ale for drink
Thou shalt have with me, O woman fair!

Omens

I heard the cuckoo, with no food in my
    stomach,
I heard the stock-dove on the top of the tree,
I heard the sweet singer in the farther copse,
I heard the screech of the night-owls.

I saw the lamb, with his back to me,
I saw the snail on his bare flag-stone,
I saw the foal, with his rump to me,
I saw the wheatear on a dike of holes,
I saw the snipe while sitting bent.

And I foresaw that the year
Would not go well with me.

The Harp

The harp to everyone is dear
Who hateth vice and all things evil;
Hail to its gentle voice so clear,
Its gentle voice affrights the Devil.

The Devil cannot the Minstrel quell:
He by the Minstrel is confounded;
From Saul was cast the spirit fell,
When David's harp melodious sounded.

She

The white bloom of the
               blackthorn, she,
The small, sweet raspberry-
               blossom, she;
More fair the shy, rare
               glance of her eye
Than the world's wealth to me.

My heart's pulse, my secret,
               she,
The flower of the fragrant apple,
               she;
A summer glow over winter snow,
'Twixt Christmas and Easter, she.

An Invocation

Bless, O Chief of generous Chiefs,
Myself and all that is near to me,
Bless me in all my actions,
Make me safe for ever,
  Make me safe for ever.

From every brownie and banshee,
From very evil wish and sorrow,
From every sprite and water-wraith,
From every fairy-mouse and grass-mouse,
  From every fairy-mouse and grass-mouse.

From every troll among the hills,
From every spirit hard-pressing me,
From every ghoul that haunts the glens,
O, save me till the end of my day,
  O, save me till the end of my day.

To the Fox that Killed his Peacock

The wretch my starry bird who slew,
Beast of the flameless ember hue,
Assassin, glutton of the night,
Mixed of all creatures that are vile,
Land lobster, fugitive from light,
You coward mountain crocodile;
With downcast eye and ragged tail
Lurking in the hollow rocks,
Thief, ever ready to assail
The undefended flocks.
Your brassy breast and shaggy locks
Shall not protect you from the hound,
When with piercing eye he mocks
Your mazy refuge underground;
Whilst o'er my peacock's broken plumes
    shall shine
A pretty bower of faery eglantine.

Epitaph on the Bard Iain Lom

Mightier was the verse of Iain,
Hearts to nerve, to kindle eyes,
Than the claymore of the valiant,
Than the counsel of the wise.

56

Index of Titles

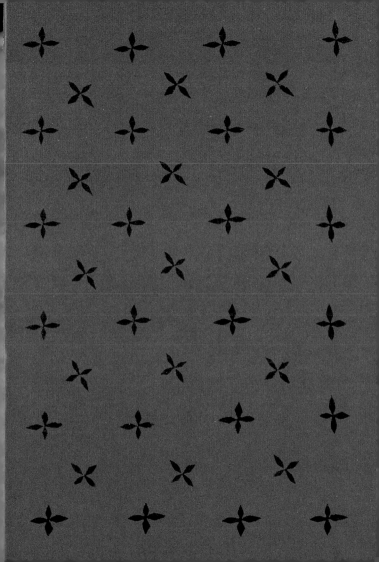

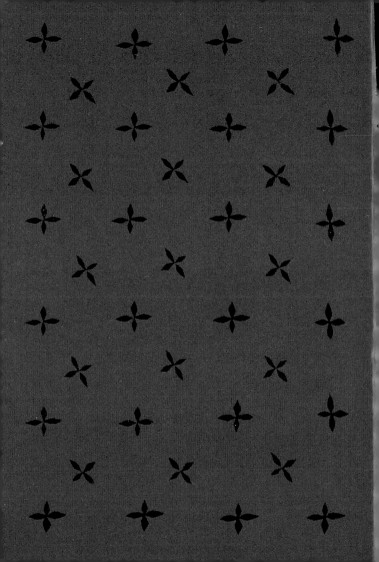